*'The Sower'* by William Johnston

New York

Van Gogh Library at Nuenen in the Netherlands

1

*Vincent Van Gogh's*

*Leap of Faith*

*Is a true story of*

*two people who are joined together*

*in time to present a Divine Story*

*of Our Heavenly Father*

ISBN 9781793988812

16th Printing July 22, 2019

# Vincent Van Gogh's
# Leap of Faith

## by William Johnston

America's Artist

**I am loved. I am a person of great worth. I am a child of God through salvation.** Lord please weave love into the very fabric of my life. Let not my time on earth be wasted or squandered on self-indulgence, but let it glow brightly with willing acceptance to listen, learn and love with passion. Many who read our little book will do so in hopes of finding answers to personal dilemmas or storms in their lives. Let those answers be a blessing from our Heavenly Father with love overflowing. These words come from a wonderland of incredible diversity. Our story is about the ebb and flow of living life to its fullest and understanding that *'This is my Father's World'* and He has expressed himself in unmistakable terms far more beautiful and breathtaking than mere language can convey. He made me in His image!

*'The Card Players' hold the key to unlocking this little book of paintings and dialog. "You are a child of God through salvation and have been dealt the most awesome winning hand. It's how you play your cards that make the difference." You are about to take a 'Leap of Faith' through award winning paintings and their story.*

*'The Card Players' by artist William Johnston*

*'Vincent Van Gogh's Leap of Faith'* is written by a man and his friend who embrace the very substance of things hoped for and the evidence of things not seen; God's love flows through its pages. Our words will bring splendor to your life. Do not be fooled by the men in orange because they are not the only ones locked up in their own prison and have lost their identity and live only for the next day. May you read and discover in gentle gratitude knowing that you are under the inspiration of His generosity. **You have been dealt a winning hand because you are a child of God through salvation. It is how you play your cards that make the difference.**

Handshake in thought,

Vincent Van Gogh and William Johnston

*Curt Kimball, MD, takes off with Leap of Faith.*

**Vincent to William**: This little book is a leap of faith.

I would want the readers of our little book to know that a plan has been recognized that when acted upon will result **in better health, wisdom in decision making, financial favor and family restoration. The Masters plan requires a *Leap of Faith*** and is the greatest story in heaven and earth. William, you did not choose me, I chose you. Most modern believers in your day have no faith structure to prepare them for an encounter like the one we are having. You allowed me to enter your world so together we can bring ministry and art to God's children in a new and refreshing way. Together we will bring closure to our combined ministries and awaken the spiritual awareness in yearning hearts. As we tell our story it would be well to let our readers know that, without knowing about me, in January of 2013, you painted a beautiful picture of the sea at sunset. William, you painted the picture for me as I watched and led. Magnificent was that experience for me. Your willing hands and my **watchful eye** came together to give a picture of our journey from earth to heaven. What a glorious experience. Little did you know that on October 31, 1876, I described such a place in my first sermon at Wesley Methodist Church. Because I love Christmas so much, let us plan to have our work completed for Christmas giving 2013. This little book will be the best gift some will ever receive. This is a love story between your Heavenly Father and His children, compassionate love. My heart is feeling the love of God in much the same way as it did when I took long walks along the Thames. Oh I long for days like those. I thought in my earthly life that one loves because one loves. I was wrong. One loves because of selfless Godly admiration that awakens like a kindled fire. It is selfless and kind. I yearned for this fulfilling experience but had great difficulty combining physical love, spiritual love and personal success together in my lifetime. Our readers may have had the same struggles. Help is near. Believe this to be so. He knows you by name.

*'Sea at Sunset' by artist William Johnston*

*Vincent Van Gogh self portrait*

**Vincent to William**: There is so much to tell. For those that lack faith in our work, they can look upon me and see my deep abiding love for my Father. Here I am in my straw hat and next to me is the Angel of Charity. We will say much about this as we describe our paintings in this precious little book. It is so beautiful here. I long for the time I was in Mr. Jones's church. Church in your time is much different. In my day most were volunteers and preaching lasted all day and often into the evening. There was something special in lighting the street lamps and singing as we warmed ourselves around the stove. I am so glad Christmas is in the winter. Our work will be complete. I asked my dear brother, Theo, to help me find a way to be in service to Our

Heavenly Father and the gospel. At one time I did not think it to be humanly possible for this to happen. God's timing is everything. A moment in time may be a hundred years to God the Father. God has chosen us for this work. I am sure of it. I knew that my request to God would be heard. God will open a way for us to proceed. What took weeks or months for me to do can now be done in the blink of an eye. William, believe me when I say God is not far. He and His Angels are very much involved in the affairs of man. Most, where I am, have put on their heavenly garment and experience love everywhere. They have no desire to put back on those earthly clothes. My petition to God has been granted for a time in this odd way. There have been many prayers requesting intercession but few believe that God is a God of his Word. I will make myself known in ways you will not be aware of to help with our little book and paintings. It seems you and I have stood the test of time and persevered. Ask and you will receive if you believe and not doubt. Believe on that as God's unfailing word.

*Many battles must be fought*

*Much of life with suffering fraught*

*Many prayers must be said*

*For a blissful end to lie ahead*

*Handshake in thought - Vincent*

*And the sower went out to sow. From Surgeon to Sower; Dr. Curt Kimball carries the sower's mission to the skies. By tractor or by plane the sower labors in the landscape of the mind and plants the good seed.*

**William to Vincent**: I can't help but think I have been truly blessed by painting our little story in pictures and reading the 91st Psalm every day for the past five years and reading it to inmates every week. I was overjoyed when I read the reading for your first sermon was the 91st Psalm. I did not see it at first but then on the fifth reading of your sermon you suggested just a little further and after the benediction there it was. I was overjoyed beyond belief. 'Ask of me and I will answer you.' 'We shall abide under the shadow of the almighty.' For a moment in time our hearts are linked together as one in His service. Remember how you reached out to the Lord with your strong commitment to serve Him. You had climbed to the mountain top and felt the very wind of Heaven. I felt so very close to God as I read your words. With your permission and blessing I would like our readers to experience firsthand your burning faith. When you preached this sermon only a handful received the blessing. Now, thousands will come to know the love of our Heavenly Father and accept him as their personal savior. I pray many will open their hearts and receive Him. May God continue to bless the hearing of His Word. I can see you as you enter the church and face the altar. I have been there many times when God's anointing has taken place. My track coach at Roswell High School, Stanley Lair, the head football coach of the Artesia Bulldogs, Cooper Henderson and Steve Thomas, crossministries.net, helped instill in me the presence of our Heavenly Father to tell them about Him the same way Jesus told Peter to

FEED MY SHEEP. These three men are perfect examples of loving what you do and walking in the steps of the Master. Oh how we need men like these to tell them about Him. Does not the day you preached this wonderful sermon seem like yesterday? The readers of our little book await the words you sent to your brother, Theo, as you remember preaching them on that marvelous day. We welcome them again after more than one hundred and thirty years. Thank you, Lord, for this gift. Vincent, paint for us in the rooms of our mind the very presence of God.

**Vincent**: I was deeply moved when I stood at the foot of the pulpit and bowed my head and prayed, "Abba, Father, in Thy name be our beginning."

**"I am a stranger in the earth, hide not Thy commandments from me." Psalm 119:19**

It is an old faith and it is a good faith that our lives are a pilgrim's progress – that we are strangers in the earth, but that though this be so, yet we are not alone for our Father is with us. We are pilgrims; our life is a long walk, a journey from earth to heaven.

The beginning of this life is this. There is one who remembereth no more her sorrow and her anguish for joy that a man is born into the world. She is our Mother. The end of our pilgrimage is the entering in Our Father's house where are many mansions, where He has gone before us to prepare a place for us. The end of this life is what we call death – it is an hour in which words are spoken, things are seen and felt that are kept in the secret chambers of the hearts of those who stand by, it is so that all of us have such things in our hearts or forebodings of such things. There is sorrow in the hour when a man is born into the world, but also joy – deep and unspeakable – thankfulness so great that it reacheth the highest Heavens. Yes the Angels of God, they smile, they hope and they rejoice when a man is born in the world. There is sorrow in the hour of death – but there too is joy unspeakable when it is the hour of death of one who has fought a good fight. There is One who has said, I am the resurrection and the life, if any man believeth in Me, though he were dead, yet shall he live. There was an Apostle, who heard a voice from heaven, saying: Blessed are they that die in the Lord for they rest from their labor and their works follow them. There is joy when a man is born in the world but there is greater joy when a Spirit has passed through great tribulation, when an Angel is born in Heaven. Sorrow is better than joy – and even in mirth the heart is sad – and it is better to go to the house of mourning than to the house of feasts, for by the sadness of the countenance the heart is made better. Our nature is sorrowful but for those who have learned and are learning to look at Jesus

Christ there is always reason to rejoice. It is a good word, that of St Paul: As being sorrowful yet always rejoicing. For those who believe in Jesus Christ there is no death and no sorrow that is not mixed with hope – no despair – there is only a constantly being born again, a constantly going from darkness into light. They do not mourn as those who have no hope – Christian Faith makes life to evergreen life.

We are pilgrims in the earth and strangers – we come from afar and we are going far. The journey of our life goes from the loving breast of our Mother on earth to the arms of our Father in heaven. Everything on earth changes – we have no abiding city here – it is the experience of everybody that it is God's will that we should part with what we hold dearest here on earth – we ourselves, we change in many respects, we are not what we once were, and we shall not remain what we are now. From infancy we grow up to boys and girls – young men and young women – and if God spares us and helps us – to husbands and wives, Fathers and Mothers in our turn, and then, slowly but surely the face that once had the 'early dew of morning' gets its wrinkles, the eyes that once beamed with youth and gladness speak of a sincere deep and earnest sadness – though they may keep the fire of Faith, Hope and Charity – though they may

### Fire of Faith

The Fire of Faith is kindled this day
By the flowers so softly given,
To teach the heart to be a part
Of a spirit never broken.


The Fire of Faith guides this hand
So lovingly touched with colors bright,
So when in need reach out and touch the
Fire of Faith
Given as He has spoken.

*by William Johnston*

beam with God's spirit. The hair turns grey or we lose it – ah – indeed we only pass through the earth, we only pass through life – we are strangers and pilgrims in the earth. The world passes and all its glory. Let our later days be nearer to Thee and therefore better than these.  Heaven is with us, helps us and guides us, gives us strength day by day, hour by hour. And so we can do all things through Christ who gives us might. We are strangers in the earth; hide not Thy commandments from us. Open Thou our eyes, that we may behold wondrous things out of Thy law. Teach us to do Thy will and influence our hearts that the love of Christ may constrain us

and that we may be brought to do what we must do to be saved. Our life, we might compare it to a journey, we go from the place where we were born to a far off haven. Our earlier life might be compared to sailing on a river, but very soon the waves become higher, the wind more violent, we are at sea almost before we are aware of it – and the prayer from the heart ariseth to God: Protect me o God, for my boat is so small and Thy sea is so great. The heart of man is very much like the sea, it has its storms, it has its tides and in its depths it has its pearls too. The heart that seeks for God and for a Godly life has more storms than any other. Let us see how the Psalmist describes a storm at sea. He must have felt the storm in his heart to describe it so. We read in the 107th Psalm," They that go down to the sea in ships, that do business in great waters, these see the works of the Lord and His wonders in the deep. For He commandeth and raiseth up a stormy wind which lifteth up the waves thereof. They mount up to Heaven, they go down again to the depth, their soul melteth in them because of their trouble. Then they cry unto the Lord in their trouble and He bringeth them out of their distresses, He bringeth them unto their desired haven."  Do we not feel this sometimes on the sea of our lives? Does not every one of you feel with me the storms of life or their forebodings or their recollections?

And now let us read a description of another storm at sea in the New Testament, as we find it in the 6th Chapter of the Gospel according to St John in the 17th to the 21st verse. "And the disciples entered into a ship and went over the sea toward Capernaum. And the sea arose by reason of a great wind that blew. So when they had rowed about five and twenty or thirty furlongs, they see Jesus walking on the sea and drawing nigh unto the ship and they were afraid. Then they willingly received Him into the ship and immediately the ship was at the land whither they went." You who have experienced the great storms of life, you over whom all the waves and all the billows of the Lord have gone – have you not heard, when your heart failed for fear, the beloved well known voice – with something in its tone that reminded you of the voices that charmed your childhood – the voice of Him whose name is Savior and Prince of peace, saying as if it were to you personally – mind to you personally 'It is I, be not afraid'. Fear not. Let not your heart be troubled. And we whose lives have been calm up to now, calm in comparison of what others have felt – let us not fear the storms of life, amidst the high waves of the sea and under the grey clouds of the sky we shall see Him approaching for Whom we have so often longed and watched, Him we need so – and we shall hear His voice, It is I, be not afraid. And if after an hour or season of anguish or distress or great difficulty or pain or sorrow we hear Him ask us 'Dost Thou love me' then let us say, Lord 'Thou knowest all things, Thou knowest that I love Thee.' And let us keep that heart full of the love of Christ and may from thence issue a life which the love of Christ constraineth. Lord Thou knowest all things, Thou knowest that I love Thee, when we look back on our past we feel sometimes as if we did love Thee, for whatsoever we have loved, we loved in Thy name. Have we not often felt as a widow and an orphan – in joy and prosperity as well and more even than under grief – because of the thought of Thee. Truly our soul waiteth for Thee more than they that watch for the morning. Our eyes are up unto Thee, o Thou who dwellest in Heavens. In our days too there can be such a thing as seeking the Lord. What is it we ask of God – is it a great thing? Yes, it is a great thing, peace for the ground of our heart, rest for our soul – give us that one thing and then we want not much more, then we can do without many things, then can we suffer great things for Thy name's sake. We want to know that we are Thine and that Thou art ours, we want to be thine – to be Christians. We want a Father, a Father's love and a Father's approval. May the experience of life make our eye single and fix it on Thee. May we grow better as we go on in life. We have spoken of the storms on the journey of life, but now let us speak of the calms and joys of Christian life. And yet, my dear friends let us rather cling to the seasons of difficulty and work and sorrow, even for the calms are treacherous often. The heart has its storms, has its seasons of drooping but also its calms and even its times of exaltation. There is a time of sighing and of praying but there is also a time of answer to prayer. Weeping may endure for a night but joy cometh in the morning.

*The heart that is fainting*
*May grow full to o'erflowing*
*And they that behold it*
*Shall wonder and know not*
*That God at its fountains*
*Far off has been raining.*

*Presentation of 'The Sower' to Farmers & Merchants National Bank, Fairview, OK*

My peace I leave with you – we saw how there is peace even in the storm. Thanks be to God who has given us to be born and to live in a Christian country. Have any of us forgotten the golden hours of our early days at home, and since we left that home – for many of us have had to leave that home and to earn their living and to make their way in the world. Has He not brought us thus far, have we lacked anything? We believe Lord, help Thou our unbelief. I still feel the rapture, the thrill of joy I felt when for the first time I cast a deep look in the lives of my Parents, when I felt by instinct how much they were Christians. And I still feel that feeling of eternal youth and enthusiasm wherewith I went to God, saying 'I will be a Christian too'.

Are we what we dreamt we should be? No – but still – the sorrows of life, the multitude of things of daily life and of daily duties, so much more numerous than we expected – the tossing to and fro in the world, they have covered it over – but it is not dead, it sleepeth. The old eternal faith and love of Christ, it may sleep in us but it is not dead and God can revive it in us. But though to be born again to eternal life, to the life of Faith, Hope and Charity – and to an evergreen life – to the life of a Christian and of a Christian workman be a gift of God, a work of God – and of God alone – yet let us put the hand to the plough on the field of our heart, let us cast out our net once more – let us try once more – God knows the intention of the spirit, God knows us better than we know ourselves for He made us and not we ourselves. He knows of what things we have need; He knows what is good for us. May He give His blessing on the seed of His word that has been sown in our hearts.

God helping us, we shall get through life. With every temptation He will give a way to escape.

Father we pray Thee not that Thou shouldest take us out of the world, but we pray Thee to keep us from evil. Give us neither poverty nor riches; feed us with bread convenient for us. And let Thy songs be our delight in the houses of our pilgrimage. God of our Fathers be our God: may their people be our people, their Faith our faith. We are strangers in the earth, hide not Thy commandments from us but may the love of Christ constrain us. Entreat us not to leave Thee or to refrain from following after Thee. Thy people shall be our people, Thou shalt be our God.

Our life is a pilgrim's progress. *I once saw a very beautiful picture*; it was a landscape at evening. In the distance on the right hand side a row of hills appearing blue in the evening mist. Above those hills the splendor of the sunset, the grey clouds with their linings of silver and gold and purple. The landscape is a plain or heath covered with grass and heather; here and there the white stem of a birch tree and its yellow leaves, for it was in autumn.

*'Sea at Sunset' by William Johnston*

Through the landscape a road leads to a high mountain far far away, on the top of that mountain a city where on the setting sun casts a glory. On the road walks a pilgrim, staff in hand. He has been walking for a good long while already and he is very tired. And now he meets a woman, a figure in black that makes one think of St Paul's word 'As being sorrowful yet always rejoicing'. That Angel of God has been placed there to encourage the pilgrims and to answer their questions:

And the pilgrim asks her:     Does the road go uphill then all the way?

and the answer is:     "Yes to the very end"–

and he asks again:     And will the journey take all day long?

and the answer is:     "From morn till night my friend".

*He said, "Tell them about Him."*

And the pilgrim goes on sorrowful yet always rejoicing – sorrowful because it is so far off and the road so long. Hopeful as he looks up to the eternal city far away, resplendent in the evening glow, and he thinks of two old sayings he has heard long ago – the one is:

'There must much strife be striven

There must much suffering be suffered

There must much prayer be prayed

And then the end will be peace.'

and the other:

'The water comes up to the lips

But higher comes it not.'

*Presentation of 'The Harvest' to Community Bank, Alva, OK*

And he says, 'I shall be more and more tired but also nearer and nearer to Thee.' Has not man a strife on earth? But there is a consolation from God in this life. An angel of God, comforting men – that is the Angel of Charity. Let us not forget Her. And when everyone of us goes back to daily things and daily duties, let us not forget – that things are not what they seem, that God by the things of daily life teaches us higher things, that our life is a pilgrim's progress and that we are strangers in the earth – but that we have a God and Father who preserveth strangers, and that we are all brethren.

Amen.

And now the grace of our Lord Jesus Christ, and the love of God, our Father, and the fellowship of the Holy Ghost, be with us for evermore.

Amen.

*'The Harvest' by artist William Johnston - Accept Jesus as your Lord and Savior and be saved.*

Scripture Reading:  Psalm 91

"He that dwelleth in the secret place of the most High shall abide under the shadow of the Almighty. I will say of the Lord, He is my refuge and my fortress: my God; in Him will I trust. Surely He shall deliver thee from the snare of the fowler, and from the noisome pestilence. He shall cover thee with His wings, and under His wings shalt thou trust: His truth shall be thy shield and buckler. Thou shalt not be afraid for the terror by night; nor for the arrow that flieth by day; nor for the pestilence that walketh in darkness; nor for the destruction that wasteth at noonday. A thousand shall fall at thy side, and ten thousand at thy right hand; but it shall not come nigh thee. Only with thine eyes shalt thou behold and see the reward of the wicked. Because Thou hast made the Lord, which is my refuge, even the most High, thy habitation; there shall no evil befall thee, neither shall any plague come nigh thy dwelling. For He shall command His angels and give them charge over thee, to keep thee in all thy ways. They shall bear thee up in their hands, lest thou dash thy foot against a stone. Thou shalt tread upon the lion and adder: the young lion and the dragon shalt thou trample under feet. *Because he hath set his love upon Me*, saith God, therefore will I deliver him: I will set him on high, because he hath known My name. He shall call upon Me, and I will answer him: I will be with him in trouble; I will deliver him, and honor him. With long life will I satisfy him, and show him my salvation."

Tossed with rough winds and faint with fear,
Above the tempest soft and clear
What still small accents greet mine ear
't Is I, be not afraid.'

't Is I, who washed thy spirit white;
't Is I, who gave thy blind eyes sight,
't Is I, thy Lord, thy life, thy light,
't Is I, be not afraid. '

These raging winds, this surging sea
Have spent their deadly force on me
They bear no breath of wrath to Thee
't Is I, be not afraid. '

*Tossed with rough winds and faint with fear, Above the tempest soft and clear, 't Is I, be not afraid. '*

14

This bitter cup, I drank it first

To thee it is no draught accurst

The hand that gives it thee is pierced

't Is I, be not afraid. '

When on the other side thy feet,

Shall rest, mid thousand welcomes sweet;

One well known voice thy heart shall greet –

't Is I, be not afraid. '

*'My Father's House' by artist William Johnston*

**William to Vincent**: I don't understand why you didn't choose one of the great artists living today. I am reminded there was a carpenter who chose local fisherman to tell the world about him. Ah - thank you for the insight. I think of the many ways our story will be told and how the paintings will remind everyone of God's love for us. Vincent, I don't know exactly what you see or what meaning it has in terms of God's plan, but I want you to know I trust in the Lord. That being said, let's invite our readers to join us in TELLING THEM ABOUT HIM through a 'Leap of Faith' where He walks with us in His garden. We are not alone.

Let's join hands and begin.

A handshake to all from Vincent and William

**Vincent to William**: I want you to know that the most important things in the world have been accomplished by people who kept on trying when there seemed to be no hope. That was me. I was not prepared or ready for the roadblocks I was to encounter as I gave myself to the Church. My road to ministry was blocked before I could really get started. Your ministry in the Methodist Church was just as intent and your gift for ministry just as real. God chose and prepared both of us for just this occasion. This opened the window of opportunity for our Heavenly Father to bring us together. We both own this understanding. TELL THEM ABOUT HIM will require both of us to bend the rule a bit, my boy. There are no secrets to success. It is the result of preparation, hard work, and learning from failure. I had plenty of failures in my day. I am pleased we are moving along. Think of it as six months painting and six months writing and the rest of your life telling them about Him. William you are a great salesman and the world is in need of our reminders. Do not be discouraged, for He is with you and you have His blessing. Tell the truth as best you know it and let the Holy Spirit do the rest. Many years ago I told my brother Theo that there were greater things in store and that time has come. My heart still burns when I hear the everlasting word of God. I so love the way we painted in your style. The masters have learned the use of brushes and devises to move paint around and how to mix colors and load their brushes to perfection but you paint with the heart of God. That's why I have chosen you to join with me on this noble mission. As God permits and you desire I will show you many new exciting things. Remember, my opening the doors of heavenly secrets is only for the purpose of glorifying our Heavenly Father. You must not fall into greed and profit taking for the things of earth. Your Heavenly Father will supply your needs. Let the world see what God is doing and they will determine what is right and good. We will tell the world about the Lamb of God and how he suffered and died for the sins of the world. Remember how the Word was made flesh and dwelt among us and the world received him not. I was so passionate about proclaiming that word and following in my father's footsteps and I suffered long and hard to no avail. It is true I mentally did myself in trying to move my friends and family to my way of thinking. It was like hitting my head against a rock. My desire for a companion and help mate brought confusion and pressure from my family and the church. I think it drove me mad. I tried to compensate for my lack of social skills by painting and taking long walks but the stress was unbearable. What sanity I had was given to me by my Heavenly Father and my brother Theo. I was a blessed man but unable to cope with the lack of acknowledgement by my peers that my work was original or even good. I have awareness that some have made large sums of money off my work and will guard like policemen the presumed value of what I could not sell in my lifetime. I find it amusing that there are no paintings in heaven, just abounding love. In Heaven we don't need to be reminded of what is. But then that is what we have captured in our little book, the stories of God's love for his people and what is. Let us say that our work shows what is to be. You will see when you get here.

**William to Vincent**: One thing I have learned from both of our lives is that we have chosen to persist until we succeed. Effort only fully releases its reward after a person refuses to quit. I look back on that beautiful golden fall day in November when our paths met and I had that urge to do what I have never done before - oil paint. I find it difficult to explain to my friends how two very strong personalities living over one hundred years apart can combine efforts to TELL THEM ABOUT HIM. Even with the facts as I know them there are only a few who believe.

*'The Sower' by artist William Johnston*

I am not discouraged. God's fire has been kindled in my heart and burns brightly. I shall continue to paint, with your guidance, the Sower, sowing the Seeds of Faith, Hope and Charity throughout the world, to all who will listen and receive. What a joy it is to sow as God prepares His soil. Oh how my heart rejoices as you bring these beautiful paintings into my life.

**Vincent to William**: As you know history has recorded my interest in Sunflowers. I spent many months laboring over these yellow creations trying to capture just the right composition. Your sunflowers capture the efforts of several distinguished painters. Let's call them CREATION. We will let the readers of our little book study the details and see how our Heavenly Father brought about these expressions of beauty. This was our beginning with a 'Leap of Faith' and so it might be for some who are trying to make some sense out of what is happening to them.

**William to Vincent:** As we begin our journey to 'Tell Them About Him,' we join our hands and hearts together and take a leap of faith by asking our readers to study our paintings very closely, for there is a divine presence you can see, if you look deep. Our Heavenly Father is watching with great anticipation how our readers play their cards.

*'Creation' by artist William Johnston*

Genesis chapter 1:27-28

27 So God created man in his own image, in the image of God created he him; male and female created he them.

28 And God blessed them, and God said unto them, Be fruitful, and multiply, and replenish the earth, and subdue it: and have dominion over the fish of the sea, and over the fowl of the air, and over every living thing that moveth upon the earth.

*Our paintings are a beautiful expression of Love for all to see and experience. They were painted for you.*

**Vincent to William:** We try so very hard to make things happen, when God is willing to create happenings for us that are bigger, better and beyond our capacity to even imagine. All of this is a matter of faith in our Father who is more than willing to provide for our every need. Remember, we are on a journey from earth to heaven. God meets our needs, not our greed's. Believe and know this to be so. I see it. Help is near. 'He shall call on me, and I will answer him.' Psalm 91

*'The Sower' by William Johnston joins University of Oklahoma 'Sower' in Sowing the good seed in the hearts and minds of all who are on that journey from earth to heaven.*

**Vincent to William:** Creation is a most interesting thought. 'In the Beginning', as is so often the case, covers a large span of time and is man's way of contemplating eternal things. You'll find when you get here that The Kingdom of Heaven is within. This is such a simple and profound part of creation. Man has learned a lot about the outer world but has yet to discover the real inner world. Jesus knew. 'Greater things than these shall you do.'

**William to Vincent:** It seems that medicine has made large strides in recent years but it still mystifies medical professionals how Lazarus was called from the grave and how the lame were made to walk or how water was turned to wine. With all his genius, man has still not learned how to get along with each other and work together for the common good.

**Vincent to William:** Change is coming.

**William to Vincent:** It is the loss of that 'child like' faith that causes us to doubt and lose trust in the magnificent work of our Heavenly Father.

**Vincent to William:** Trust will lead us to places where we can only imagine. Remember how your nine year old granddaughter painted a peacock for Cody and Lacey's wedding. This was trust as your Heavenly Father meant it to be. You were amazed at her ability as were others. If only mankind could realize that it is this child like faith that produces such outstanding results.

*'Peacock' as painted by nine year old Kassidy Brianne Pameticky, granddaughter of artist William Johnston*

**William to Vincent:** I was amazed at Kassidy's insights and attention to detail. I watched as she held her brush and selected her paints. I noticed how steady her hand was and how her heart was set on doing something wonderful for her uncle Cody and Lacey. There is more to be said here about creation than we understand.

*Farmers Exchange Bank of Cherokee, Oklahoma receives a framed print of the oil painting 'Seasons.' "To everything there is a season, and a time to every purpose under the heaven."*

**Vincent to William:** There were many parts of creation that I did not understand. It was only later that I began seeing the art work of Claude Monet, Pierre Auguste Renoir, and Cezanne as creative genius. The mystery and intrigue behind these artists is magnified by time, but all realized why they were created and made every effort to express themselves. Cezanne painted numerous paintings of card players, but none had the story idea of your inmate's playing cards and how they became the subjects of our little book of paintings and dialog.

**William to Vincent**: God blessed His creation and sanctified it. Then He rested. Much can be learned from the Bible that tells us about God and ourselves. How wonderful it is that we can remind the readers of our little book through our paintings of what our Father has done for His children. As you know both of us have had to develop self-discipline to complete these inspired paintings for our little book. If we are to succeed in telling them about Him we both will need to apply all the self-discipline we can, without it our mission is impossible. Early in your life you were full of passion and dedicated to great success in service to God's people. Your first sermon I read often with excitement as if I were a child in my mother's arms listening to her read a bedtime story. Then, over the years you became beat down and unclear of which direction to go. Something changed in you. Your inner light became dimmer and dimmer. I see and feel it in my spirit. I feel the same toward the inmates in our picture, The Card Players. I believe it to be the loss of SPIRITUAL PROSPERITY. The road uphill became more difficult and your steps grew slower and slower. Your self-image became a heavy weight on your shoulders. Nothing I know of more affects a person's demeanor than to not have the necessities of life. We get so down on ourselves that we cannot think. Am I going to die or live? I see you as you paint the Bible and by it a candle whose light has been extinguished. My heart aches for you in your struggle but I see it and the world sees it for many who read our little book can identify with you. I feel enlivened with God's spirit as I know confessions are being made and people are praying for help with their unbelief. Are we not in a constant struggle to overcome the world and find peace with God? I think of Jesus in the Garden of Gethsemane. The struggles he had to overcome were so much greater than ours. I think it is our struggles that bind us together. There are many. How can it be that our paths can be so similar that time has joined us together without regard to time or space? I realize how our lives share the same emotions and mental anguish as well as a pulling from God to serve Him with all our heart, soul and mind. I look at our pictures and I am amazed, simply amazed. How beautiful. What an everlasting story of joy and love. My inner self glows when I look at them. I see the spirit of God, the hand of my Heavenly Father, the movement of time towards a great goal; I see the one who made you and me. I am grateful and humbled. The fire of God burns brightly within my body. I pray our little book will be successful the way God intends it.

**Vincent to William**: You need not worry about our success. It seems history has made much to-do about a man who only sold one of his paintings during his lifetime. I remember the dark days when I painted with very little light and my colors weren't as bright as yours. If it weren't for my brother Theo and a few friends I would have ceased to exist. By the way, history didn't get it right about my last days. Theo knows. You are right about those days of despair. It seemed to me that everyone I loved turned against me. It isn't that I didn't have a real job; I had lost the motivation to move in any direction. Many reading our story will identify with that feeling. All that was made worse by the fact that I had given away most of my worldly possessions save for a few paintings, drawings and pieces of art which were my only lifeline. My worldly belongings were few and my food was scarce. I gave most of my paintings away and the rest I could not sell. Theo and some others tried but there just wasn't any interest. I think if the truth were known there are a lot of people who go through the same experience. **That is why I know our little book and paintings will encourage people to have faith and hold on to the light of Christ which will illuminate the way to eternal life.** I am thinking of John Wesley's little book of sermons, "How to get to heaven and land safely on that happy shore." Not much is said these days about being born again. Revive us again my boy!

**William to Vincent**: I'm sure the history books and the curators of your effects, with raised eyebrows of course, will want to hear your own version of what happened in July 1890. I will depend on your inspiration and guidance, for surely there will be a doubting Thomas amongst our readers. While I was in seminary at Southern Methodist University I wrote a Credo, what I believed. It was nothing like this. I have many of our paintings on one wall so I can see them and experience each one every day. I have to admit that a picture does say a thousand words. My oldest son Ryan asked, "Where did this come from?" When he reads our little book he will know. My youngest son Cody says I have reached down deep. My daughter Amy says she is amazed. I must say I am blessed. I am blessed. God has embraced me with a heavenly embrace and joined me to a brother who dares to ask for the impossible and believes it to be so.

**Vincent to William**: I'm sure there will be an out pouring of views and opinions. I asked Theo to guard this time with the utmost care. He was a faithful and sometime only real supporter I had. It's like our Heavenly Father who after creation found he didn't have many supporters for all he had created. That is except for a man named Noah. Remember the rainbow? You didn't understand our painting at first. Then, with a slight nudge, there it was, a modern day Noah with an age old story. It is best the people reading our little book revisit God's Promise.

The world was evil and corrupt in the time of Noah. He was a righteous man and the **only** follower of God left on the earth. The Bible says he was blameless among the people of his time. It also says he walked with God and pleased Him. William, the story of Noah is vital to our story.

*'Noah' by artist William Johnston*

**Genesis: 9:12-13**  God makes His covenant with man.

12 And God said, This is the token of the covenant which I make between me and you and every living creature that is with you, for perpetual generations:

13 I do set my bow in the cloud, and it shall be for a token of a covenant between me and the earth.

*'The Tree of Knowledge of Good and Evil'*
*by artist William Johnston*

**William to Vincent:** The story of Noah is about choices between good and evil. Our Heavenly Father wants us to make good choices because we love Him and choose to obey Him. The tree of the knowledge of good and evil reminds us of the consequences of making the wrong choices. Noah made good choices and did as God instructed and was not separated from God. Making right choices is about 'How we play our cards' and obedience.

**Vincent to William:** There are consequences for making wrong choices. Our readers know. We are free to make wrong choices, as were Adam and Eve. There are a great many temptations in the world which bring about sin and separate us from God and keep us from obtaining eternal life. That is why our Heavenly Father found it necessary to send His son to die on the cross because of our wrong choices. God loves His children and has given them yet another choice of acceptance. That is why we are writing our little book to 'Tell them about Him.'

**William to Vincent:** We are children of God through salvation and nothing can change that. The story of Noah serves as a constant reminder of a Father's love for His children. I think as we tell our readers about Him we will have to include our friend Moses. I was inspired by Renoir and his wonderful talent for expression. I became so caught up in the obvious that I almost missed the most important point. Life is a little that way. Things are rarely as they seem. I felt your presence as I filled in the background for our picture the second time. As I finished I stood back and there they were, Moses with the Ten Commandments and all the Israelites dressed in the robes of their day. I noticed how you emphasized remembering the commandments.

Moses

'Moses' by artist William Johnston

Moses

Reading the

10 Commandments

EXODUS 20:1 And God spoke all these words, saying: "I am the Lord your God, who brought you out of the land of Egypt, out of the house of bondage.

1. You shall have no other gods before me.
2. You shall not make for yourself any carved image, or any likeness of anything that is in heaven above, or that is in the earth beneath, or that is in the water under the earth; you shall not bow down to them nor serve them. For I, the Lord your God, am a jealous God, visiting the iniquity of the fathers on the children to the third and fourth generations of those who hate me, but showing mercy to thousands, to those who love Me and keep My commandments.

3. You shall not take the name of the Lord your God in vain, for the Lord will not hold him guiltless who takes His name in vain.
4. Remember the Sabbath day, to keep it holy. Six days you shall labor and do all your work, but the seventh day is the Sabbath of the Lord your God. In it you shall do no work: you, nor your son, nor your daughter, nor your manservant, nor your maidservant, nor your cattle, nor your stranger who is within your gates. For in six days the Lord made the heavens and the earth, the sea, and all that is in them, and rested the seventh day. Therefore the Lord blessed the Sabbath day and hallowed it.
5. Honor your father and your mother, that your days may be long upon the land which the Lord your God is giving you.
6. You shall not murder.
7. You shall not commit adultery.
8. You shall not steal.
9. You shall not bear false witness against your neighbor.
10. You shall not covet your neighbor's house; you shall not covet your neighbor's wife, nor his manservant, nor his maidservant, nor his ox, nor his donkey, nor anything that is your neighbor's."

**William to Vincent**: It does seem you have willed yourself into my life. I don't know how you were able to accomplish this but I'm sure our readers would like to know. It would appear that people fail to reach their fullest potential in knowing our Heavenly Father because they lack the will to do the things that others refuse to do. If we don't make our Heavenly Father our habitation this whole business of religion becomes blurred and unclear. I remember how you gave me the inspiration to paint, "Through a Glass Darkly." Oh how I love it so.

*'Through a Glass Darkly' by artist William Johnston*

1 Corinthians Chapter 13

13 Though I speak with the tongues of men and of angels, and have not charity, I am become as sounding brass, or a tinkling cymbal.

[2] And though I have the gift of prophecy, and understand all mysteries, and all knowledge; and though I have all faith, so that I could remove mountains, and have not charity, I am nothing.

[3] And though I bestow all my goods to feed the poor, and though I give my body to be burned, and have not charity, it profits me nothing.

[4] Charity suffers long, and is kind; charity envies not; charity boasts not itself, is not puffed up,

[5] Does not behave itself unseemly, seeks not her own, is not easily provoked, thinks no evil;

[6] Rejoices not in iniquity, but rejoices in the truth;

[7] Bears all things, believes all things, hopes all things, endures all things.

[8] Charity never fails: but where there be prophecies, they shall fail; where there be tongues, they shall cease; where there be knowledge, it shall vanish away.

[9] For we know in part, and we prophesy in part.

[10] But when that which is perfect is come, then that which is in part shall be done away.

[11] When I was a child, I spoke as a child, I understood as a child, I thought as a child: but when I became a man, I put away childish things.

[12] For now we see through a glass, darkly; but then face to face: now I know in part; but then shall I know even as also I am known.

[13] And now abides faith, hope, charity, these three; **but the greatest of these is charity**.

**William to Vincent:** As you know this painting didn't start out this way. It was a gift of God.

**Vincent to William**: I do understand my boy. Many of my paintings became do-over's. I had to make the most of my supplies and so I painted over many of my canvases. I have to admit our little painting turned out better than I expected. A perfect representation of how the Apostle Paul saw Jesus. Oh if the world could see Paul now. There are many here in heaven that you will see in that grand and glorious day. Jesus is more beautiful than I could have ever imagined. Love abounds in this place called Heaven. Remember how tedious it was to paint the perfect petals. God in all his glory basking in heavenly sunshine awaits those who view our little cherry tree in full bloom. You might recall the vision of my little almond tree. This was a fun painting in my particular style. You will see when your time on earth is complete that history has a way of making things larger than life.

*'Heaven' by artist William Johnston*

**William to Vincent**: God knows us as we are and He knows our needs. We are blest. Can you feel the hand of your Heavenly Father embracing you? Many times during my life I felt the hand of God directing my life and lifting me higher and higher to better see the things of our Heavenly Father. I believe reading the 91st Psalm every day has drawn me into a relationship that has not only allowed us to create our story book of dialog and paintings but to experience Heaven on Earth. Vincent, as people read our little book they will know that someone is praying for them and that they are not alone. Believe with all your heart and doubt not that this is so.

Matthew Chapter 5: The Sermon on the Mount

Now when Jesus saw the crowds, he went up on a mountainside and sat down. His disciples came to him, [2] and he began to teach them.

**The Beatitudes**

He said:

<sup></sup>3 "Blessed are the poor in spirit,
   for theirs is the kingdom of heaven.
<sup></sup>4 Blessed are those who mourn,
   for they will be comforted.
<sup></sup>5 Blessed are the meek,
   for they will inherit the earth.
<sup></sup>6 Blessed are those who hunger and thirst for righteousness,
   for they will be filled.
<sup></sup>7 Blessed are the merciful,
   for they will be shown mercy.
<sup></sup>8 Blessed are the pure in heart,
   for they will see God.
<sup></sup>9 Blessed are the peacemakers,
   for they will be called children of God.
<sup></sup>10 Blessed are those who are persecuted because of righteousness,
   for theirs is the kingdom of heaven.

*When seed fell on good soil, it grew, yielding thirty, sixty, and a hundredfold.*

*'Creede, CO' by artist William Johnston*

11 "Blessed are you when people insult you, persecute you and falsely say all kinds of evil against you because of me.

12 Rejoice and be glad, because great is your reward in heaven, for in the same way they persecuted the prophets who were before you.

**William to Vincent**: I have spent sixty six years trying to figure out this thing called success. I now know that success is so much more than money and status. One should not try to become a person of success, but rather try to become a person of value. Success will be determined by what others say about you. Time has taught me the real value of friendships. Friends are a gift.

I think of aspen leaves quaking in the summer breeze of Creede, Colorado and my friend R. Deane Wymer and my physician Dr. Don Klinger, whose mission is to tell them about Him in Uganda, East Africa and my friend Larry Jensen as he sang 'How Great Thou Art' at the altar of the United Methodist Church and Merle Patzkowsky as he teaches FAITH to those who hunger and thirst every Saturday morning. It is I, be not afraid. Be strong and believe.

**Vincent to William**: An inspiring and refreshing thought. As we tell them about Him it is important to remind the readers of our little book the importance of learning. I often reminded Theo about visiting museums and learning about art and artists. There is a season for everything, as we so aptly captured in our fall scene in the woods. I remember my many walks along the Thames as seasons changed and there were such beautiful fall colors.

Remember how Solomon wrote the little book of Ecclesiastes? He made many mistakes in his life, just like many of our readers and decided to document them. He wrote his book so future generations would not have to suffer and live in misery seeking after materialistic things, but rather offered wisdom by discovering truth in seeking after God. This is the same reason we are writing our little book and asking our readers to consider the lessons revealed to us by our Heavenly Father so their lives will be better.

*'Seasons' by artist William Johnston*

Ecclesiastes Chapter 3

1 To everything there is a season, and a time to every purpose under the heaven:

2 A time to be born, and a time to die; a time to plant, and a time to pluck up that which is planted;

3 A time to kill, and a time to heal; a time to break down, and a time to build up;

4 A time to weep, and a time to laugh; a time to mourn, and a time to dance;

5 A time to cast away stones, and a time to gather stones together; a time to embrace, and a time to refrain from embracing;

6 A time to get, and a time to lose; a time to keep, and a time to cast away;

7 A time to rend, and a time to sew; a time to keep silence, and a time to speak;

8 A time to love, and a time to hate; a time of war, and a time of peace.

**William to Vincent**: I am glad to find you haven't lost your enthusiasm. So often people meet failure head on and soon the end comes. It is said that 'Success is the ability to go from one failure to another with no loss of enthusiasm.' What a great insight and inspiring thought since you and I have experienced this first hand. You and I have our dreams. This little book is 'a dream come true' for those who are willing to dig deep and listen to that still small voice. Dreams come true if we have the courage to pursue them.

**Vincent to William**: Diligence my boy. There are those who believe in good luck when diligence brings about the right result. We need to ask God for a place to find meaning in our lives. I spent many inspiring moments quietly reflecting on my struggles. My brother Theo was always eager to receive my simple drawings in my letters explaining my struggles. We all need a place. That is why we should be reminded of the Psalmist who asks, "Lead me beside the still waters." I recall the clear reflective lake in our painting "Still Waters."

*'Still Waters' by artist William Johnston*

Psalms Chapter 23

1 The LORD is my shepherd; I shall not want.

2 He maketh me to lie down in green pastures: he leadeth me beside the still waters.

3 He restoreth my soul: he leadeth me in the paths of righteousness for his name's sake.

4 Yea, though I walk through the valley of the shadow of death, I will fear no evil: for thou art with me; thy rod and thy staff they comfort me.

5 Thou preparest a table before me in the presence of mine enemies: thou anointest my head with oil; my cup runneth over.

6 Surely goodness and mercy shall follow me all the days of my life: and I will dwell in the house of the LORD forever.

**William to Vincent**: A handshake for now. Take time for a few moments of reflection.

One of my favorite pastimes is fishing the lakes and streams in Colorado. As a boy I remember watching in quiet anticipation for some unsuspecting trout to rise to my fly and then want to be free more than I wanted him in my creel. It is that same feeling I have as we cast our net on the other side of the boat. We are to become great fishers of men. A way will be provided for a bountiful harvest.

*'Reflections' by artist William Johnston*

**William to Vincent**: What do you think of our work thus far?

**Vincent to William**: I spent a lot of time working with artists of my day. It was my hope to improve my style and learn the secrets of the masters. Finally I came to the conclusion it's all in the eye of the beholder. Remember our blue vase with flowers and what happened when you began putting centers in the flowers? It shocked me when I too began seeing all the faces in the painting. Yes indeed, beauty is in the eye of the beholder just as love is in the heart of the beholder. The more time you spend in it the more you see. Well done William.

**William to Vincent**: I have spent many hours gazing at 'Eye of the Beholder.' I have watched the faces of others as they stand and gaze, and then all of a sudden I hear them begin to describe one face and then another and another. Making God our habitation draws us into many experiences in the same way. At first we may not see or understand them but then it comes to us as the work of our Heavenly Father. God is a great and good God. He brings many such experiences to our lives so that we may love Him all the more. He touched me, this I know.

*'The Eye of the Beholder' by artist William Johnston*

**William to Vincent**: I am overwhelmed with the progress we have made. People have many experiences when it comes to knowing the Lord. I remember my early beginnings in Kiowa, Oklahoma. On a trip to McAlester, Oklahoma there were several of us in my old car. Out of the stillness of the moment she began to sing acapella, "Nearer My God to Thee." Chills came over me. I have never known anyone to have such perfect pitch. The world would come to know her as Reba. I knew her as a child of God with a wonderful gift.

**Vincent to William**: I have had many such experiences. Finding the Lord was the greatest of these. I wish everyone could have an Emmaus Road experience. Paul was blinded; others looked into a burning bush or were called forth from the grave. I think your mountain scene describes where you met the Lord and your wonderful loving wife Janice.

**William to Vincent:** Meeting someone you love or being in a place where life changing events happen create lasting memories. I have always believed that good memories and good habits are needed to replace the bad ones. So I ask our readers to see themselves walking along our mountain road breathing fresh mountain air and knowing that God is with them, even now.

*'The Emmaus Road' Cloudcroft, New Mexico by artist William Johnston*

**William to Vincent**: This experience with you has taught me to risk going too far. I had no idea I could do this or have this experience. Only those who risk going too far can possibly find out how far they can go. I am wondering why you have not led me to paint more in your style? I know you painted the Raising of Lazarus after Rembrandt and the Reaper with Sickle after Millet. I would very much like to know about your drawings, backgrounds and the kinds of brushes you used. Perhaps this is something you would teach me if I could somehow better communicate with you. I love your use of colors and shadows. Please tell me how you load your brush and the use of outline for your subjects. I have been studying the feet of your subjects, how they are moving with the picture. I am anxious to try. I do not want to distract the readers of our little book so please, in the quiet still moments, stir within me this great art form. I see new stories developing for what is next. How exciting. I can see your frustration with not having paints and canvas when inspiration comes on you. I can feel your heart when you continually have to ask for supplies. Ask of me and I will answer you. Supplies came and your work flourished. This is a difficult experience for those caught in the stresses of life. I would remind the readers of our little book that the road up hill and the road down are one and the same. We are challenged to do the things we are afraid to do. We need purpose and direction. Success in life can never be an accident. It is the result of right decisions at the right time.

Champions are not people who never fail, but people who never quit. I can see the improvement in your never quit style and your attention to detail as in Red Chestnut in the Public Park at Arles. It is very moving. If I could only have been there with you, we would have made a great team. Come to think of it, we are a Great Team. I am going to Creede, Colorado, this summer and I shall take photos of this old silver mining town and apply what I am experiencing. Your Restaurant de la Sirene at Asnieres will serve as my example of brush strokes and lighting. You are right. Our future will be very exciting. I can see why lack of peer support would have been deflating. I know everyone who has examined your life as tried to figure you out.

**Vincent to William**: My life has been examined by layman and professionals alike. None of them understand that my life was not complete and my ministry and painting were not finished. I am doing what no-one in history has ever done. My mission is to "Tell Them About Him." I SEE IT and I KNOW IT TO BE TRUE. It is my hope to call laborers for the Lord, those who would tell them about Him. That is why we painted "The Harvest." The harvest is plentiful but the laborers are few. Matthew 9:27

*'The Harvest' by artist William Johnston*

**William to Vincent:** I thought of your sermon as I painted the Harvest. It is the storms in our lives that test our belief and cause us to doubt. As sure as day follows night there will be storms. It is such a beautiful experience to go to the Lord and, with love in your heart, ask and see what God will do for those who ask Him.

Where I live we have just finished wheat harvest. It was so beautiful watching the green stems turn golden and then tipping their heads toward the ground as if giving thanks to God.

Luke 10:2

"Therefore said he unto them, the harvest truly is great, but the laborers are few: pray ye therefore the Lord of the harvest, that he would send forth laborers into his harvest."

**Vincent to William**: It is my resolution to succeed at this one thing. Thank you for your willingness to be there for me. My paintings would all be for naught if I failed to finish the race set before me. It seems that I passed many failures on the way to true success. I am that pilgrim described in my sermon. I know you feel the excitement of a totally new experience. The hint of combining our efforts is exciting for me too. But let us not forget the purpose of our little book. When we have completed this leg of our work there will be a long uphill climb through the jails and prisons. As a matter of fact it may not happen in your lifetime. Many things are set in stone and the political system is slow to move on things like this. We must practice the presence of God. My coming to you will be enough for some to open doors. When we are finished we can say we did what we were commissioned to do. The heavenly angels will rejoice with every sinner who repents and there will be jubilation in heaven. Let us keep running the race that is set before us.

*'You are Loved' by artist William Johnston*

**William to Vincent**: There are those who think they can run the race and those who think they can't, they are both right. I can see myself along your road with cypress and star. The sky is intriguing. We should make our faith invitation just as inviting. I was wondering what Jesus thinks about our work? Can I ask such a bold question? Many would like to know.

**Vincent to William**: You are loved. All will not see it. But there, the King of Kings, the one whose name is above all names gave Himself on the cross for you. That is why you and I are given the challenge to tell them about Him. There is a lot to do and the world is moving very fast. Time will tell.

**Vincent to William:** The trouble with our world is that people don't realize that Jesus loves them as if they were the only one. He has given to them all that is needed, Father, Son and Holy Spirit. That's why I gave to you, "Trinity." As we work through writing this little book remember that everyone is a pilgrim on this earth searching for faith; faith in something or someone. We all experience frustrating times and our faith begins to collapse. Even Elijah had to pray seven times and David had ashes on his head many a time. When this happens to me I think of my wonderful family and friends who loved me so or I take a walk in one of my many favorite places. I can hear the church bells ringing along the Thames on Sunday morning or smell the beautiful green grass. We lack not for clear visions of God's accomplishments. I do believe church bells are a thing of the past and few would know the sound of a harmonium. I do have a bit of trouble balancing time. I am so pleased with our paintings. Many will be warmed and enlivened by their beauty. We must trust with that faith of old. Make happy memories as you reflect on our mission and tell them about Him. Remember, pictures will be filling your head and your heart that must be expressed in drawings or paintings. I will bring people to you who are eager to provide material for your painting and I encourage you to invite them into this process. More is happening than you know. Keep telling them about Him. The word is getting out.

**William to Vincent:** I can tell you that as we painted Trinity the paint flowed from my brush. I could feel the spirit of God coming over me. I dedicated this painting to you in the name of the Father, and the Son and the Holy Spirit. Our readers need to know God as Father, Son and Holy Spirit. Our readers will be known by the fruit they bare. Our Heavenly Father freely gives us fruit of the spirit beginning with LOVE, JOY and PEACE. Galatians 5:22

*'Trinity' by artist William Johnston*

**Vincent to William:** Now you know why I have come to you, to tell them about Him. I don't know that anyone has ever dedicated a painting to me. I thank you and feel blessed. This is a most unusual experience to have a painting dedicated to oneself.

Accept in thought a handshake, and believe me,

your loving friend,

Vincent


**William to Vincent**: I must say it was a special evening when Doyle Riley gave that invitation to Christian discipleship on December 25th, 1966. I sat at the back of Aldersgate Methodist Church and received Jesus as my Lord. I knew then that Jesus shed his blood for me and with tears running down my cheeks answered the call. I will call this red vase painting, "A Red Vase with Flowers" and remember that Jesus died for me and for a world of lost sinners.

*'A Red Vase with Flowers' by artist William Johnston*

**Vincent to William**: I can't begin to describe to you where I am so that the world would understand. Let me just say that I am in the presence of my Heavenly Father. My heart rejoices with you as we present our little painting to those who would receive it. Just as people receive different gifts of the spirit, they also come to know Jesus in different ways. For some the road will be blocked because they will feel the price is too high or they have to give up too much. There is much joy and happiness in knowing the Lord. Those in heaven know.

**William to Vincent**: When Jesus told Peter to "Feed My Sheep" He was saying, "Tell them about me." I see it! It is instilled in my mind.

John 21

15 So when they had dined, Jesus saith to Simon Peter, Simon, son of Jonas, lovest thou me more than these? He saith unto him, Yea, Lord; thou knowest that I love thee. He saith unto him, Feed my lambs.

16 He saith to him again the second time, Simon, son of Jonas, lovest thou me? He saith unto him, Yea, Lord; thou knowest that I love thee. He saith unto him, Feed my sheep.

*'The Grand Finale' by artist William Johnston*

17 He saith unto him the third time, Simon, son of Jonas, lovest thou me? Peter was grieved because he said unto him the third time, Lovest thou me? And he said unto him, Lord, thou knowest all things; thou knowest that I love thee. Jesus saith unto him, Feed my sheep.

**William to Vincent:** I call this painting 'The Grand Finale.' Jesus is coming again. I embrace every reader with that loving thought. You are invited to His table to participate in His eternal banquet. God has prepared a place for you, a place like no other, your eternal home in heaven.

38

**William to Vincent**: I long for the perfect embrace for the readers of our little book. They need it so desperately. There is a crossing over from the old to the new. There was a crossing over when you painted the Seine Bridge at Asnieres. Few have noticed that you painted yourself in that picture in much the same way you painted yourself in mine. You are casting your net into the sea. You are waiting. Here am I send me. I will tell them about Him.

Revelation Chapter 21: The New Jerusalem

1 And I saw a new heaven and a new earth: for the first heaven and the first earth were passed away; and there was no more sea.

2 And I John saw the holy city, new Jerusalem, coming down from God out of heaven, prepared as a bride adorned for her husband.

3 And I heard a great voice out of heaven saying, Behold, the tabernacle of God is with men, and he will dwell with them, and they shall be his people, and God himself shall be with them, and be their God.

4 And God shall wipe away all tears from their eyes; and there shall be no more death, neither sorrow, nor crying, neither shall there be any more pain: for the former things are passed away.

5 And he that sat upon the throne said, Behold, I make all things new. And he said unto me, Write: for these words are true and faithful.

6 And he said unto me, It is done. I am Alpha and Omega, the beginning and the end. I will give unto him that is athirst of the fountain of the water of life freely.

7 He that overcometh shall inherit all things; and I will be his God, and he shall be my son.

**William to Vincent**: Thank you Vincent for your determination to proclaim the Word and "TELL THEM ABOUT HIM."

**Vincent to William** and the readers of our little book: The Success of what we have done here will not be measured by our paintings or by our dialog but by the obstacles our readers will overcome. We have torn down a wall to the past and built a bridge to the future. We will build a firm foundation for God with the bricks that are thrown at us. We have a firm resolution to succeed in our mission. We must remember that being defeated is often a temporary condition. Giving up is what makes it permanent. William let me say as we bring our little book to a close, our friend and companion John Wesley proclaimed, "Today I set myself on fire and you have come to watch me burn." That is what we have done. Your Heavenly Father saw your heart as you lovingly read the 91st psalm year after year and answered the call to tell them about Him. This is only a beginning. **More is to come as our readers take the time to discover what God**

**has in store for them as they read the 91st Psalm every day. That is the plan we recognized as we began this journey with a LEAP OF FAITH. It's all in how you play your cards.** I give you a handshake in thought for you to pass along to others as you tell them about Him. This is the dawning of a new day. I see it. I know it to be so.

We invite our readers to join us for the Grand View and contemplate your place in God's majestic plan. A place has been prepared for you among these stones for you to sit and experience the love and power of the Almighty. Stay awhile and come back often, for the presence of God is in this place.

*'The Grand View' by artist William Johnston*

# Psalm 121

I lift up my eyes to the hills.
From where does my help come?
My help comes from the Lord,
who made heaven and earth.

"In six days God created the heaven and the earth. And the earth was without form, and void; and darkness was upon the face of the deep. And the Spirit of God moved upon the face of the waters. And God said, Let there be light: and there was light. And God saw the light, that it was good: and God divided the light from the darkness. And God called the light Day, and the darkness he called Night. And the evening and the morning were the first day." Genesis 1:1-5

*'A Journey in Time' by artist William Johnston*

'Heaven's Gate' by artist William Johnston

"I am the way, the truth and the life.  No one comes to the Father but by me." Jesus, the Son of God. John 14:6

## The Sending of the Sower

Don Klinger, DO, and William Johnston send the SOWER to Uganda, East Africa.

Medical care is scarce. Teams work day and night, often in primitive conditions, doing what they can.

A few receive life-saving operations while most can only hope that Team Hope will come their way.

*Uganda Team Hope consists mostly of doctors, nurses and ministers. They are glad to be sowers of the Good Seed of their faith, hope and charity.*

*The children come with thankful hearts from nearby villages in hope of receiving the lifesaving love and attention they so desperately need.*

*'Church in the Valley' by artist William Johnston*

He's Been Waiting

Welcome to the Church in the valley. Come on in, the doors are open and the lights are on. A place has been reserved just for you. He's been waiting.

"Amazing Grace, how sweet the sound, that saved a wretch like me....

I once was lost but now am found, was blind, but now, I see."

John Newton (1725-1807)

**William to Vincent:** It is with outstretched arms that our readers are invited to explore the greatest mystery of all time. Why were we created and for what reason did our Heavenly Father make us in His image? The answer is found not by reading but by doing. It is in our generosity and helpfulness, especially toward the needy and suffering, that we begin to see what the Son of God teaches us through His life and ministry. The tie that binds us to our Creator is the practice of **charity.** This is the voluntary giving of help to those in need who are not related to us. **May the Angel of Charity guide and watch over us as we explore _'Charity'_ as the pure love of God.** It is beautiful.

_Charity_

_'The Angel of Charity'_
_by artist William Johnston_

**Vincent to William:** Now we must take another 'Leap of Faith.' Our readers will see _charity in action_ as described by the apostle who wrote to so many churches of his day. Until we unlock life's purpose with the key of Charity we haven't gained access to the real understanding of its importance. Once again, it is how our readers play their cards that make the difference. This will be a new experience for many and one that will test the very foundation of their belief. I thought that giving the world art and artist, who painted pictures of our Heavenly Father's love, would convey the necessity of charity. I experienced many difficulties since it seemed I had little to give. In my early days I encountered coal miners and their families who had very little of anything and barely existed. I tried to express this in my painting, 'The Potato Eaters,' but most did not understand or care for its dark drab colors nor understood what it meant to have so little.

**William to Vincent:** The Angel of Charity is the bond that unites us in a divine mission. Our paintings have given us a Biblical accounting of who we are as children of our Heavenly Father. We see ourselves on that journey from earth to heaven, sowing good seeds along the way. It is the expected harvest from our sowing that will provide the abundance from which others will experience God's love in a tender and caring way. I have adorned these pages with flowers from 'My Father's House,' so everyone can experience their beauty and reach down deep for understanding.

**Vincent to William:** It is difficult to reach down deep, for it is like looking in a mirror, we see ourselves as we really are. As we discover what we are saved from, we are called to look at what we are saved for. That is why we need the Angel of Charity with us. As people look in the mirror, do they not see hard-heartedness, pitilessness, ruthlessness, hate, viciousness, or harshness in their lives? As they look again they might see reprisal, retaliation, meanness or spite lurking in the shadows. Heaven has none of these things. I find it interesting that charity increases as income decreases. Much is said about this in God's Holy Word. Take time to reflect on these things and you will better understand the difficult situation we are in and why we have come to you. Take time to be Holy as you paint for us the presence of the Almighty. Without Charity we cannot inherit that place prepared for us in our Fathers house. Charity qualifies us for the Lord's work. Know this to be so. Continue to sow the good seed. A harvest is coming.

**William to Vincent:** It is sin that so easily besets us. We are pleasure seekers in a world of takers and abusers. The body is a temple and should be treated as such. We should seek the Light. My Heavenly Father shall fill us with light as we journey through time. Charity reveals the light from above. It is beautiful.

**Vincent to William:** It is a marvelous thing, that our lives should be aglow with the light of Christ. This light allows us to see Godly things more clearly and decide where to spend our time and money. The impoverished, particularly those widowed or orphaned, and the ailing or injured, are generally regarded as the proper recipients of charity. These people who cannot support themselves and lack outside means of support sometimes become beggars, directly soliciting aid from strangers encountered in public. Remember how Jesus told us, "Whatever you did not do for one of the least of these, you did not do for me." Matthew 25:45 Judgment will be too late, we must tell them about Him.

'Go Tell It On The Mountain'
Aglow with the light of Christ.
by artist William Johnston

**William to Vincent:** The readers of our little book think of charity as providing basic necessities such as food, water, clothing, healthcare and shelter, but other actions are charity as well: visiting the imprisoned or the homebound, educating orphans, even social movements. Donations to causes that benefit the unfortunate indirectly, such as donations to fund cancer research and the work of Lions Clubs or our work in Uganda, East Africa are also charities.

**Vincent to William:** Charity as the pure love of Christ is the love that Christ has for us and that we should have for one another. It is the highest, noblest, and strongest kind of love and the most joyous to the soul.

**William to Vincent:** May the God of our habitation bless our little book and provide light to illuminate the way.

*"Ask of me and I will answer you." Psalm 91*

*2013 Book Signing at Hastings Book Store, Enid, Oklahoma*

*"I will give unto him that is athirst of the fountain of the water of life freely." Revelations 21:6*

*William Johnston*
*United Methodist Minister 1971 - 1996*

The inspiration for LEAP OF FAITH came to me in November of 2012 from a spiritual awakening to tell the story of our Heavenly Father through oil paintings. I told my wife, Janice, of forty-four years, about this experience and asked her for a Christmas gift of paints, canvases, brushes and an easel. I had no idea how I was going to do this, but I knew there would be a way provided. Little did I know there was an artist who lived one hundred thirty seven years ago who would enter my life and help me fulfill this undertaking. Vincent Van Gogh, at an early age, developed a passion for ministry from his father and studied to become a Methodist minister, only to find his efforts were blocked due to the lack of language and math skills when he attempted to enter seminary.

Vincent Van Gogh's life was stormy to say the least. His brother, Theo, was his main financial supporter since he was only able to sell one of his paintings during his short lifetime. I found there to be two very dramatic circumstances taking place; the door to Van Gogh's ministry was blocked by the church and his life as an artist never received the recognition or endorsement by his peers that he desired.

All of this came to me when I began painting the 'Sea at Sunset.' It took me two tries to sense what was happening to me. As I looked at the finished painting, there he was, looking at me as if from the grave. It was from this very moment that I began having the thought, 'Tell Them about Him.' The 'Him' I felt I understood; it was the 'Them' that I didn't get at first. The dialog and paintings in our little book tell the story of an incredible relationship developed between two people who share the same passion, to 'Tell Them about Him' and take a LEAP OF FAITH. It was the inmates in jail who became the subjects of my painting, 'The Card Players.' They were the 'Them' in my understanding of 'Tell Them about Him.' To the best of my knowledge I have been faithful to this calling and await the opportunity to share this story with as many as who will hear it. I feel this is only a beginning. I pray those who hold the keys to telling this story will allow it to be heard by those who so desperately need to experience the love of our Heavenly Father in this tender way. They will get it. 'Everyone has been dealt a winning hand through salvation, it's how they play their cards that make the difference.' I believe deep down all this is the result of reading the 91st psalm every day and asking the Lord to allow me to live my life for Him. 'He shall call upon me, and I will answer him, says the Lord.' **I call this *a miracle of faith*.**

Everyone won't 'get it' or think this little book of paintings and dialog is of any great importance. Some will.  And for that reason I give you, 'Vincent Van Gogh's - Leap of Faith.' Van Gogh gave us truth and color and in his own way an understanding of eternal life. Perhaps your heart will be strangely warmed and you too will become a voice in the Great Commission.

A handshake in thought,

William Johnston

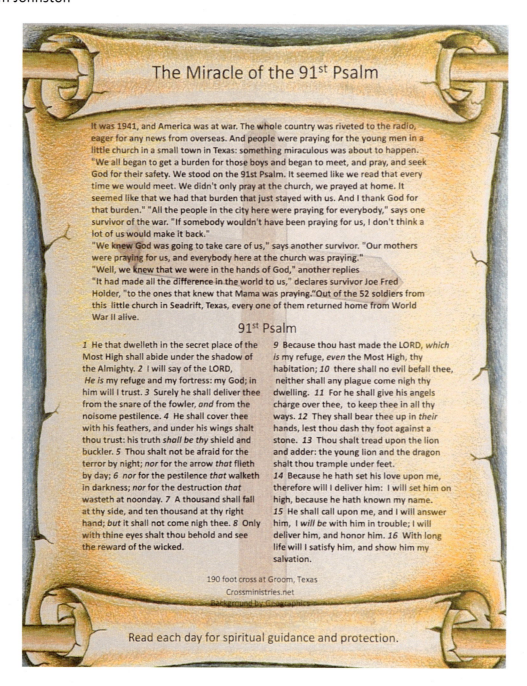

## The Miracle of the 91st Psalm

It was 1941, and America was at war. The whole country was riveted to the radio, eager for any news from overseas. And people were praying for the young men in a little church in a small town in Texas: something miraculous was about to happen. "We all began to get a burden for those boys and began to meet, and pray, and seek God for their safety. We stood on the 91st Psalm. It seemed like we read that every time we would meet. We didn't only pray at the church, we prayed at home. It seemed like that we had that burden that just stayed with us. And I thank God for that burden." "All the people in the city here were praying for everybody," says one survivor of the war. "If somebody wouldn't have been praying for us, I don't think a lot of us would make it back."
"We knew God was going to take care of us," says another survivor. "Our mothers were praying for us, and everybody here at the church was praying."
"Well, we knew that we were in the hands of God," another replies
"It had made all the difference in the world to us," declares survivor Joe Fred Holder, "to the ones that knew that Mama was praying."Out of the 52 soldiers from this little church in Seadrift, Texas, every one of them returned home from World War II alive.

### 91st Psalm

1 He that dwelleth in the secret place of the Most High shall abide under the shadow of the Almighty. 2 I will say of the LORD, *He is* my refuge and my fortress: my God; in him will I trust. 3 Surely he shall deliver thee from the snare of the fowler, *and* from the noisome pestilence. 4 He shall cover thee with his feathers, and under his wings shalt thou trust: his truth *shall be thy* shield and buckler. 5 Thou shalt not be afraid for the terror by night; *nor* for the arrow *that* flieth by day; 6 *nor* for the pestilence *that* walketh in darkness; *nor* for the destruction *that* wasteth at noonday. 7 A thousand shall fall at thy side, and ten thousand at thy right hand; *but* it shall not come nigh thee. 8 Only with thine eyes shalt thou behold and see the reward of the wicked.

9 Because thou hast made the LORD, *which is* my refuge, *even* the Most High, thy habitation; 10 there shall no evil befall thee, neither shall any plague come nigh thy dwelling. 11 For he shall give his angels charge over thee, to keep thee in all thy ways. 12 They shall bear thee up in *their* hands, lest thou dash thy foot against a stone. 13 Thou shalt tread upon the lion and adder: the young lion and the dragon shalt thou trample under feet.
14 Because he hath set his love upon me, therefore will I deliver him: I will set him on high, because he hath known my name. 15 He shall call upon me, and I will answer him, I *will be* with him in trouble; I will deliver him, and honor him. 16 With long life will I satisfy him, and show him my salvation.

190 foot cross at Groom, Texas
Crossministries.net
Background by Geographics

Read each day for spiritual guidance and protection.

Books may be purchased from Amazon.com, Bookstores and Online Retailers, Libraries and Academic Institutions, Amazon Europe and sent directly as a gift or to the jail or sheriff in your area. You can make a difference by *Telling Them about HIM.*

Ask for
# Vincent Van Gogh's 'Leap of Faith' by William Johnston

Translations will become available as they are completed.

To find a jail address in your area go to: http://www.countyjailinmatesearch.com/(name of state)

Suggested placements for 'Leap of Faith':

College Students

Nursing Homes

Hospitals

Hotels and Motels

Doctor's offices

Giving Occasions

Offices

Libraries

Churches

Casinos

Bars

Clubs

Restaurants

Airlines

Trains

*Presentation of 'Church in the Valley' to Community National Bank – Fairview, OK*

*Major County Historical Society book signing, 'Vincent Van Gogh's Leap of Faith'*

# The Sower's Story

*And the Sower went out to sow.*

Your journey, with a 'Leap of Faith' will be amazing. Be assured the Angel of Charity will abide with you. Your responsibility is to sow the good seed; your Heavenly Father will watch over it and provide for it and bring it to harvest. Daily reading the 91$^{st}$ Psalm will protect and guide you. The Angel of Charity will provide light unto your path, a path that leads to your home in heaven. Take time to be Holy, speak often with the Lord. Find a Bible based church and grow your faith. Life is short.

It is a journey from earth to heaven. We are bringing our picture book to you so you can become part of the sower's story and a voice in the Great Commission. Remember, Jesus holds the future, He is in control and there will be a day of judgment. We should be reminded of the Four Horseman of the Apocalypse. There is still time for the unbelievers to turn to Jesus and away from sin. We have painted for you God's merciful love in giving you yet another chance to turn to him before the final judgment. There will be a time when the earth trembles and everyone will face the judgment of the Lamb. Experience charity, pray the sinner's prayer and know the love of your heavenly father.
**Vincent and William**

*May the Lord bless you and keep you. And may our little book of paintings be a light unto your path that leads you home.*

# Sinners Prayer

*"Father, I know that I have broken your laws and my sins have separated me from you. I am truly sorry, and now I want to turn away from my past sinful life toward you. Please forgive me, and help me avoid sinning again. I believe that your son, Jesus Christ died for my sins, was resurrected from the dead, is alive, and hears my prayer. I invite Jesus to become the Lord of my life, to rule and reign in my heart from this day forward. Please send your Holy Spirit to help me obey You, and to do Your will for the rest of my life. In Jesus' name I pray, Amen."*

If you decided to repent of your sins and receive Christ today, welcome to God's family. Now, as a way to grow closer to Him, the Bible tells us to follow up on our commitment.

- Be baptized as commanded by Christ.
- Tell someone else about your new life in Christ.
- Spend time with God each day. Develop the daily habit of praying to Him and reading His Word. Ask God to increase your faith and your understanding of the Bible.
- Seek fellowship with other believers. Develop a group of believing friends to answer your questions and support you.
- Find a local Bible based church where you can worship.

## Stormy Stormy Night
### by William Johnston

There's a Lighthouse shining brightly through the stormy stormy night, so that all who see its beacon know it shines forever bright. The storms of life continue, as I journey on, while the light from that old lighthouse guides this old ship home. Years of stormy nights have taken their earthly toll, but through all those storms it still stands, through wind and rain, to have one goal. Those whose lives are tempest tossed can know that on a stormy stormy night they can lift their eyes to heaven and see the light that leads them home. I am thankful that Jesus is my lighthouse, he's my rock and fortress from on high. His guiding light has shown around me so these old eyes can have eternal sight. As the storms of life are raging I'm drawn nearer my God to thee, for my home in heaven is my final destination and on that happy shore I plan to be.

Poem dedicated to Vincent Van Gogh and Robert Deane Wymer

*'Stormy Stormy Night' by artist William Johnston*

I dedicate our little book to my father,

## Charles Johnston

for his dedication and devotion to the 91st Psalm.

May our Heavenly Father bless the telling and hearing of this story.

William Johnston - wrjart@yahoo.com - www.wrjart.com

*The Church at Auvers is an oil painting created by Dutch post-impressionist artist Vincent van Gogh in June 1890 which now hangs in the Musée d'Orsay in Paris, France. The actual church is in Place de l'Eglise, Auvers-sur-Oise, France, 27 kilometres north-west of Paris.*

***Café Terrace*** *at Night by William Johnston.* ***Café Terrace*** *at Night is a **1888** oil painting by the Dutch artist Vincent van Gogh in **1888**. It is also known as The Cafe Terrace on the Place du Forum, and, when first exhibited in 1891, was entitled Coffeehouse, in the evening (Café, le soir).*

# The Star
## of Bethlehem

*Now when Jesus was born in Bethlehem of Judaea in the days of Herod the king, behold, Wise-men from the east came to Jerusalem, saying, "Where is he that is born King of the Jews? for we saw his star in the east, and are come to worship him. "In Bethlehem of Judaea: for thus it is written through the prophet, "And thou Bethlehem, land of Judah, Art in no wise least among the princes of Judah: For out of thee shall come forth a governor, Who shall be shepherd of my people Israel."   Matthew 2:1-12*

*Vincent Van Gogh's Chair*

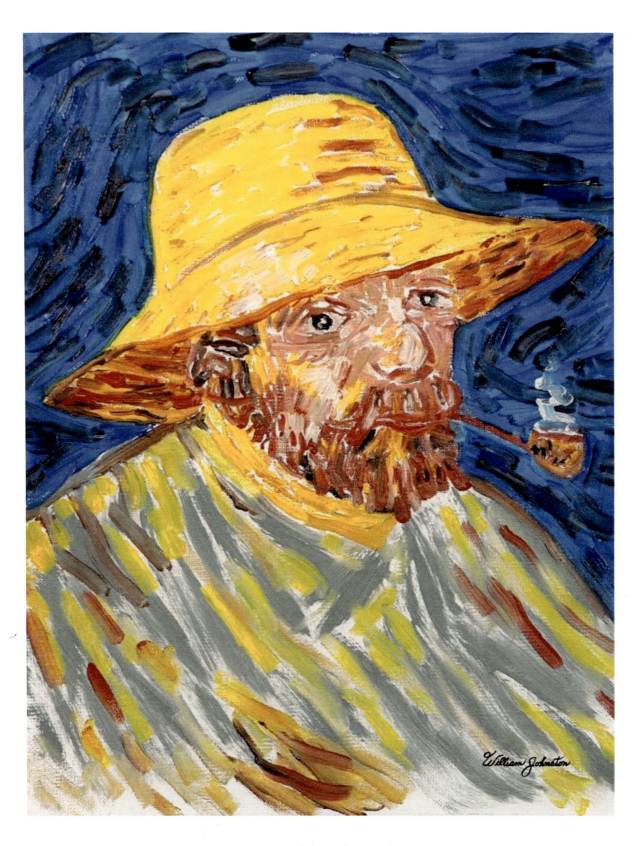

*Vincent Van Gogh by William Johnston*

"He that dwelleth in the secret place of the Most High shall abide under the shadow of the Almighty."

Psalm 91:1

"It is an old faith and it is a good faith that our lives are a pilgrim's progress – that we are strangers in the earth, but that though this be so, yet we are not alone for our Father is with us. We are pilgrims; our life is a long walk, a journey from earth to heaven." Vincent Van Gogh

*William and Janice Johnston*

*May the Lord bless you and keep you. And may 'Vincent Van Gogh's Leap of Faith' be a light unto your path that leads you home.*

*Vincent Van Gogh*

**by artist William Johnston**

# When Time Stopped

I don't expect anyone to believe what I am about to write, it will sound like something from "Believe it or not". It is a continuation of a spiritual adventure called Vincent Van Gogh's 'Leap of Faith', published in 2013. This story begins when I heard a television commercial telling of the upcoming movie, 'Lust For Life,' featuring Kirk Douglass and Anthony Quinn. The movie time was announced for 7 PM on Turner Classic Movies. I was home early that evening where I sat in my favorite rocker and waited for the movie to air. As 7 PM approached I remember looking at the wall clock. When at last the movie came on I looked, again, at the clock. The time was still 7 PM. I thought the clock had simply stopped, for I noticed on several occasions the clock still read 7 PM. What happened some 122 minutes later at the end of the movie is what really caught my attention. When the movie ended, the clock started again. I remember telling my wife and a few friends. The next morning I woke up early at 4:30 AM and once again clicked on the TV to find a segment featuring how the movie 'Lust for Life' was made.

Perhaps I should start from the beginning so my readers can fully understand the meaning of this happening. It all started in 2002, when my dad introduced me to a story about a WW2 experience at Sea Drift, Texas where 52 soldiers were prayed for by the residence of this small town, praying the 91$^{st}$ Psalm every day. The story tells how all fifty two men came home from the war alive. Thus begins my story of reading the 91$^{st}$ Psalm every day.

The first eight years were some-what uneventful. Then little things would happen to me that gave me the feeling of being near to my divine Father. It was in the tenth year that something truly amazing happened. In the fall of 2012 I experienced an overwhelming sensation of wanting to paint. I explained to my wife that something came over me and I needed to paint pictures. I asked her to buy me the needed supplies as a Christmas gift. On Christmas morning there they were, a good supply of oil paints, several 16" X 20" canvases, an easel, brushes, a pallet and paint thinner. Little did I know what was in store for me as I set up my easel with canvas and laid out my paints in my home office. Now what do I do? Then, as if divinely guided, I told myself I would paint the sea at sunset. Without a picture or video to guide me I began. There was nothing magical about this painting and I said to myself, "it's not bad, but it's not good either." By this time I realized oil paints take time to dry, so I found a place on the living room floor where my table mounted easel could sit and be out of the way for a few days. Each morning I would sit in my rocker and stare at my new painting. Why was I led to begin this new journey?

On the third day, as I looked at my painting, I noticed there was an unusual silhouette appearing from the picture of a person looking straight at me. I told my wife there was what appeared to me a picture of a face in the painting. Who was this mysterious face? What did this have to do with this new found venture? I decided to do a little research on self-portraits by artists who painted themselves looking straight at you. As I studied various artists I came across one image of an impressionist painter named Vincent Van Gogh. It did look similar to my painting and, once again, I told my wife of my fascination with this relationship. Who was this post-impressionist Dutch painter? What relationship would my humble painting have to do with Van Gogh?

Since all of this seemed to come out of the blue, I was intent on finding out more; especially, did it have anything to do with the 91$^{st}$ Psalm. I began studying the person of Vincent Van Gogh in an attempt to discover what all this meant. This is where my story becomes surreal. I found several on-line videos of Van Gogh and began watching and learning why this was happening to me.

I discovered that Van Gogh wanted to be a Methodist Minister early in his life but found his way to be a rocky road. Try as he may, the church found him to be unacceptable and chose not to allow him to enter seminary. Since I am a retired United Methodist Minister I can feel deeply for such a rejection. This is where I learned that a lot of what Van Gogh did he communicated in writing with his brother Theo. This is where I was led to the many letters Van Gogh wrote to Theo concerning his trials and tribulations with the church. One such letter contained his first sermon preached at Wesley Church in London, England. As I read the manuscript I thought to myself, "How beautiful." About two thirds of the way through the sermon it happened. In his sermon he stated that, "Life is a pilgrim's progress. I once saw a very beautiful picture. It was a landscape at evening. In the distance on the right hand side a row of hills appearing blue in the evening mist. Above those hills the splendor of a sunset, the gray clouds with their linings of silver and gold and purple. The landscape is a plain or heath covered with grass and heather; here and there the white stem of a birch tree and its yellow leaves, for it was autumn." This was an exact description of my painting. Cold chills came over me as I continued to read. A sermon beautifully written concluding with a familiar benediction, "And now may the grace of our Lord Jesus Christ, and the love of God, our Father, and the fellowship of the Holy Ghost, be with us for evermore. Amen" What came next told me why all this happened to me. The scripture reading for Van Gogh's first sermon was Psalm 91.

I described this whole series of events in my book, Vincent Van Gogh's Leap of Faith" as follows, "The inspiration for LEAP OF FAITH came to me in November of 2012 from a spiritual awakening to tell the story of our Heavenly Father through oil paintings. I told my wife, Janice, of forty-four years, about this experience and asked her for a Christmas gift of paints, canvases, brushes and an easel. I had no idea how I was going to do this, but I knew there would be a way provided. Little did I know there was an artist who lived one hundred thirty seven years ago who would enter my life and help me fulfill this undertaking. Vincent Van Gogh, at an early age, developed a passion for ministry from his father and studied to become a Methodist minister, only to find his efforts were blocked due to the lack of language and math skills when he attempted to enter seminary. Vincent Van Gogh's life was stormy to say the least. His brother, Theo, was his main financial supporter since he was only able to sell one of his paintings during his short lifetime. I found there to be two very dramatic circumstances taking place; the door to Van Gogh's ministry was blocked by the church and his life as an artist never received the recognition or endorsement by his peers that he desired.

All of this came to me when I began painting the 'Sea at Sunset.' It took me two tries to sense what was happening to me. As I looked at the finished painting, there he was, looking at me as if from the grave. It was from this very moment that I began having the thought, 'Tell Them about Him.' The 'Him' I felt I understood; it was the 'Them' that I didn't get at first. The dialog and paintings in our little book tell the story of an incredible relationship developed between two people who share the same passion, to 'Tell Them about Him' and take a LEAP OF FAITH. It was the inmates in jail who became the subjects of my painting, 'The Card Players.' They were the 'Them' in my understanding of 'Tell Them about Him.' To the best of my knowledge I have been faithful to this calling and await the opportunity to share this story with as many as who will hear it. I feel this is only a beginning. I pray those who hold the keys to telling this story will allow it to be heard by those who so desperately need to experience the love of our Heavenly Father in this tender way. They will get it. 'Everyone has been dealt a winning hand through salvation; it's how they play their cards that make the difference.' I believe deep down all this is the result of reading the 91st psalm every day and asking the Lord to allow me to live my life for Him. 'He shall call upon me, and I will answer him, says the Lord.' **I call this *a miracle of faith*.**

Everyone won't 'get it' or think this little book of paintings and dialog is of any great importance. Some will. And for that reason I give you, 'Vincent Van Gogh's - Leap of Faith.' Van Gogh gave us truth and color and in his own way an understanding of eternal life. Perhaps your heart will be strangely warmed and you too will become a voice in the Great Commission."

A handshake in thought,

William Johnston

   The result of the dialogue between Van Gogh and me was the painting of God's story in simple pictures beginning with "The card Players" and ending with "The Open Bible." "Leap of Faith" is a true story of two people who were joined together in time to present a Divine story of our Heavenly Father."

*Sunflowers by William Johnston*

I have been obedient to this calling. Upon completion of "Vincent Van Gogh's Leap of Faith" I was shown yet another form of painting which was new to me and new to the world. I wondered why I was not led to paint in Van Gogh's style. I was told, "As God permits and you desire I will show you many new and exciting things." I was warned that "my opening the doors of heavenly secrets is only for the purpose of glorifying our Heavenly Father. I must not fall into greed and profit taking for the things of this world. Therefore one half of all profits made from the production of these new paintings will be given to Lions Club International where serving humanitarian needs helps those who need it most. Money will be given to help teach adults, who cannot read, in third world countries, learn to read. Van Gogh's mission was to help the lost and outcasts of society. Therefore I will contribute to those causes that do the most good in society.

What was to come next was a total surprise. Everything I had painted up to now I understood. I had rented the third floor of the old I Tower hotel in Fairview, Oklahoma and set up a "Gallery of the South" where I could paint and write. This was good and well, but I had no room to do larger canvases. I remembered going to the fifth floor which was empty, no heat or electricity, no air conditioning, no water or bathrooms and most of all no ventilation.

It was late spring when I decided to try this new space and see what happened. I didn't understand that all these situations had to be in place to create the Van Gogh style art. I soon discovered that I needed special legs on my canvases which were on the floor, to move my canvases and get the needed effect. I had a vision one night and saw exactly how to create these canvas stilts. I took my idea to a friend, Marvin Martens, and asked him to make them for me. He did. And they were perfect. So, with all my supplies, I headed to the fifth floor. By now it was approaching early summer and the room was around ninety degrees mid-day. This is when the unexpected happened. As I applied the paint, sweat from my forehead would drop into the paint and create beautiful designs as I moved the canvas. It was so hot I could only work a few hours at a time. This was the beginning of a new swirling Van Gogh art form. The paintings were truly different. They were beautiful, but no one wanted these strange new art paintings.

Why was I given this strange new technique? My paintings were exhibited in New York, Dallas, Santé Fe, Oklahoma City and while interesting, only a few sold. By this time I had met several professional artists who told me not to be discouraged. By this time I felt I had been given an artistic style that was ahead of its time. I had fallen into the proverbial trap, all out go and no income. Thankfully my day job kept me going. In fact it was my job as president and Executive Director of MAGB Transportation that gave me the answer to my dilemma. I had several high mileage vans that looked good but needed to be retired. My thought was to use them as a mobile billboard and place them where people would see them and know who to call. How could I use my new paintings as a mobile billboard?

As I thought about this there popped up on my computer screen "Wear Your Art," by DIVA. DIVA had created all the templets to apply to all kinds of clothing as well as a way to manufacture, sell and advertise through face book. This was a long way from where I started. But now you know how I got to where I am today. The next generation art delivered to the world in a matter of seconds.

God works this way. He can do things you haven't even thought of yet. The 91st Psalm tells us to make God our habitation, ask of Him and He will answer you. Remember Van Gogh sold only one painting during his short lifetime and now millions of people will be wearing his inspired art and funding the projects most dearest to his heart.

Knowing that you're wearing a proclamation is an amazing thing. Like the disciples of old who heard a voice saying "follow me." I give to you what has been given to me, a gift from the Father. From drops of sweat to divine design. DIVA for future generations.

The *INVITATION* by William Johnston

Please take a few moments and look into the eyes of Vincent Van Gogh and see if his message touches you or your loved ones. Vincent had a difficult time communicating his feelings of love and caring all of his life and found that the best way to accomplish this was through his paintings.

For me, this is only a beginning. I continue to read the 91st Psalm every day, looking for answers to the age old problem of sin. There are many unanswered questions about living life to its fullest and having the necessities to carry on everyday living. Some of you know what I mean.

This I know, as I painted this portrait from one of Van Gogh's self-portraits I could feel his hands on mine, moving the brush, wanting the message contained in this little book of paintings and dialogue to be understandable to anyone who comes to this reading as a little child. There is much yet to be done, and miles and miles to go before I rest. Perhaps you will pick up the torch and carry our message onward and make God your habitation, for He will show you His salvation.

Vincent and William

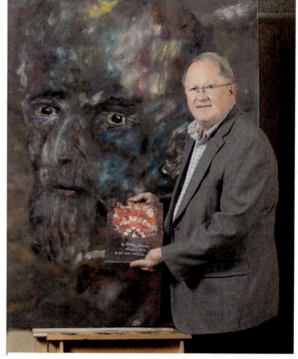

*Oil painting of Vincent Van Gogh 2016 with artist William Johnston and his book, 'Vincent Van Gogh's Leap of Faith,' available on Amazon.*